Deschutes
Public Library

C.3

SUPER
SANDCASTLE
Super Simple Crafts

SUPER SIMPLE
Glass Jar Art

Fun and Easy-to-Make
Crafts for Kids

Karen Latchana Kenney

Consulting Editor, Diane Craig, M.A./Reading Specialist

ABDO
Publishing Company

Published by ABDO Publishing Company, 8000 West 78th Street, Edina, Minnesota 55439. Copyright © 2010 by Abdo Consulting Group, Inc. International copyrights reserved in all countries. No part of this book may be reproduced in any form without written permission from the publisher. Super SandCastle™ is a trademark and logo of ABDO Publishing Company.

Printed in the United States.

Editor: Liz Salzmann
Content Developer: Nancy Tuminelly
Cover and Interior Design and Production: Oona Gaarder-Juntti, Mighty Media
Photo Credits: Colleen Dolphin, Shutterstock
Activity Production: Oona Gaarder-Juntti

The following manufacturers/names appearing in this book are trademarks: Elmer's® Glue-All®, Goo Gone®, Reynolds® Cut-Rite® Waxed Paper, Target® Aluminum Foil

Library of Congress Cataloging-in-Publication Data

Kenney, Karen Latchana.
  Super simple glass jar art : fun and easy-to-make crafts for kids / Karen Latchana Kenney.
    p. cm. -- (Super simple crafts)
  "Tools and Supplies Find the Jars Prepare the Jars Super Savings Banks Pet Treat Jar Wacky Monster Snowman Jar Picture Paperweight Magic Mosaic Jar Nature Light Super Snow Globe Glossary."
  ISBN 978-1-60453-624-9
  1. Glass craft--Juvenile literature. I. Title.

TT298.K4654 2010
748.5--dc22
                        2009000352

Super SandCastle™ books are created by a team of professional educators, reading specialists, and content developers around five essential components—phonemic awareness, phonics, vocabulary, text comprehension, and fluency—to assist young readers as they develop reading skills and strategies and increase their general knowledge. All books are written, reviewed, and leveled for guided reading, early reading intervention, and Accelerated Reader® programs for use in shared, guided, and independent reading and writing activities to support a balanced approach to literacy instruction.

To Adult Helpers

Making art from glass jars is fun and simple to do. There are just a few things to remember to keep kids safe. There are some activities where adult supervision is recommended. Also, there will be sticky and oily liquids used in some activities. Make sure kids protect their clothes and work surfaces before starting.

Table of Contents

Tools and Supplies. 4

Find the Jars 6

Prepare the Jars 7

Super Savings Banks. 8

Pet Treat Jar 10

Wacky Monster 12

Snowman Jar. 16

Picture Paperweight 18

Magic Mosaic Jar 22

Nature Light 24

Super Snow Globe 28

Glossary 32

Symbols

Look for these symbols in this book.

Super Hot. Be careful! You will be working with something that is super hot. Ask an adult to help you.

Adult Help. Get help! You will need help from an adult.

Fun With Glass Jars!

Did you know a glass jar can become art? It's true! Make a snow globe or a candle holder. It's simple! To begin, find some cool glass jars. Make sure you wash them well! Then try some or all of the fun **projects** in this book. It's up to you! From start to finish, making super simple glass jar art is fun to do!

Tools and Supplies

Here are many of the things you will need to do the **projects** in this book. You can find them online or at your local craft store.

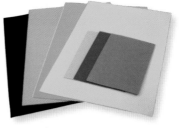

craft foam sheets

construction paper

paintbrushes

pom-poms

acrylic paint

coins

polymer clay

jars

colored sand

decorative stickers

ribbon

foam letters

clear packing tape

fabric

mineral oil

rubber bands

cookie sheet

foam paintbrush

aluminum foil

plastic confetti

candle

hole punch

tissue paper

florist's clay

glue

glitter

wax paper

electrical tape

pipe cleaners

googly eyes

Find the Jars

Before you start your art, you need the right glass jar!

- Look for jars that have different shapes.

- Look in the kitchen for jars that are almost empty. Ask an adult if you can use them.

- Check out your glass recycling bin. Be sure to wear gloves to protect your hands while looking in the bin.

- Test the jars to make sure their lids fit tightly. Put some water in a jar and screw on the lid. Hold the jar over the sink or take it outside. Then shake the jar. If no water comes out, you've found a good jar!

Prepare the Jars

Glass jars need some work before they can become art!

Clean the Jars

1. Empty out the jar.

2. Clean the jar and lid with dish soap and warm water.

3. Take off the label. If it doesn't all come off, soak the jar in hot, soapy water. After 10 minutes, try peeling the label off again. If it still won't come off, soak it some more. You can also use a product such as Goo Gone. Ask an adult for help.

4. Let the jar and lid dry completely.

Paint the Lids

A jar may have a logo or other **design** on its lid. You can paint the lid to cover up the logo. You will need newspaper, acrylic paint, and a paintbrush.

1. Decide which **project** you want to make.

2. Paint the outside of the lid. Do not paint the inside.

3. Set the lid on some newspaper to dry. If the logo shows through the paint, paint it again. Let the paint dry completely.

Super Savings Banks

Small change can add up fast when you save it in cool jars!

Supply List

- 4 jars with metal lids
- electrical tape
- construction paper
- scissors
- marker
- clear tape
- coins (1 of each type)
- white paper
- crayons or colored pencils
- glue

1. If the lids need to be painted, follow the steps on page 7. Ask an adult to make coin **slots** in the lids. If the edges are sharp, cover them with electrical tape.

2. Cut a strip of construction paper to wrap around each jar. Write the types of coins on the strips.

3. Tape one end of a strip to the side of a jar. Wrap the strip around the jar and tape the other end. Repeat this step for the other jars.

4. Put a coin under a piece of white paper. Rub over the coin with a crayon or colored pencil. Keep the paper and coin still while you are rubbing. Make 8 to 12 rubbings of each coin. Try using different colors and both sides of the coins.

5. Cut out the coins and glue them onto the jars. Make sure you put the correct coins on each jar! Screw on the lids and start saving!

Pet Treat Jar

your pet will love to get treats from a yummy-looking jar!

Supply List
- a jar with a lid
- glue (optional)
- foam letters
- decorative stickers
- pet treats

1. If the lid needs to be painted, follow the steps on page 7.

2. Use foam letter stickers to spell your pet's name. Stick them across the middle of the jar.

3. Choose some fun stickers. Put them on the jar around your pet's name. You might need to use glue to help them stick.

4. You can decorate the lid with more stickers.

5. Fill the jar with your pet's favorite treats!

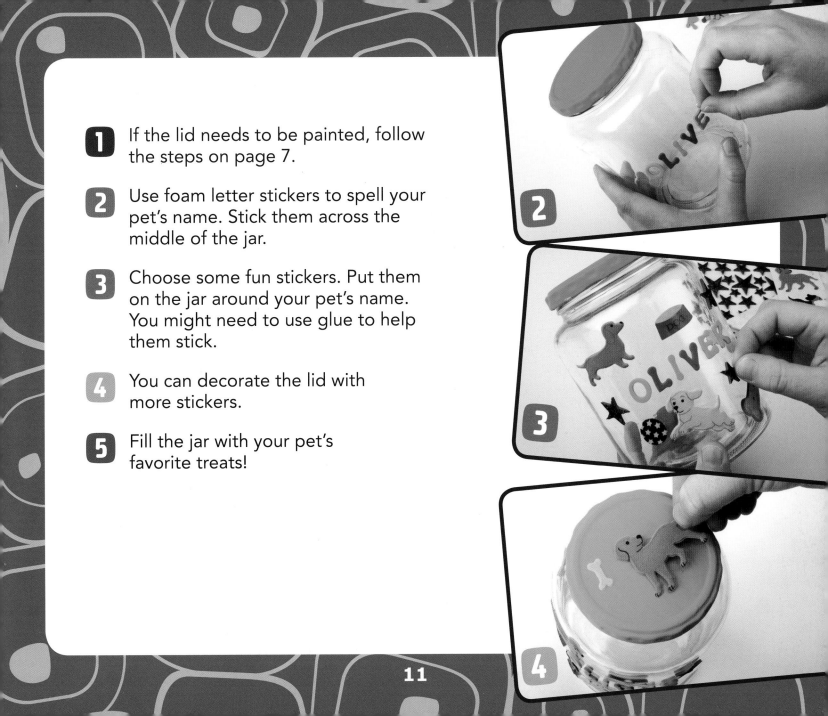

Wacky Monster

your friends will laugh at this funny monster face!

1. If the lid needs to be painted, follow the steps on page 7.

2. Ask an adult to use a hammer and a nail to make two holes in the lid.

3. Choose two pipe cleaners. Wrap each pipe cleaner around a pencil and then slide it off. Now they look like springs!

4. Glue a googly eye to one end of each pipe cleaner.

5. Push the other end of each pipe cleaner through a hole in the lid. Bend the ends of the pipe cleaners. This will keep them from coming out of the holes. There might be sharp edges by the holes, so be careful.

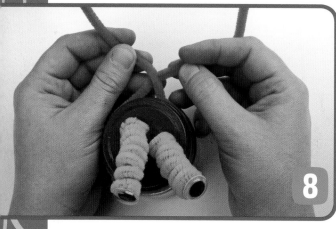

6 Fill the jar with pom-poms. You can use one color or a mix of colors. Screw on the lid.

7 Choose two pipe cleaners for the arms. Twist the pipe cleaners together to make a **really** long pipe cleaner.

8 Wrap the long pipe cleaner around the jar under the lid. Twist the pipe cleaner so it stays around the jar. Pull the ends apart so they stick out like arms.

9 Cut two hand shapes out of foam. Push the end of each pipe cleaner through the bottom of a hand. Fold the ends of the pipe cleaners and twist them under the hands.

More Super Ideas

Try decorating your monsters in different ways.

Snowman Jar

This snowman will keep marshmallows fresh!

Supply List

- jar with a lid
- googly eyes
- glue
- black and orange craft foam
- scissors
- black marker
- hole punch
- marshmallows

1. If the lid needs to be painted, follow the steps on page 7.

2. Glue two googly eyes onto the jar. Hold them in place until the glue sets. This might take a few seconds.

3. Cut a carrot shape out of orange foam for the nose. Draw three little black lines on it with the marker. Glue the nose under the eyes.

4. Use a hole punch to make little circles of black foam. Glue the circles to the jar in the shape of a mouth.

5. Cut three circles out of black foam for the buttons. Glue them to the jar.

6. Cut a top hat out of black foam. Glue the hat onto the side of the lid.

7. Wait for the glue to dry. Then fill the jar with **marshmallows**.

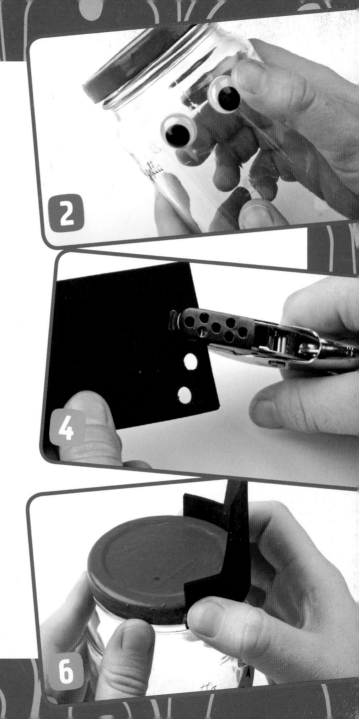

Picture Paperweight

A great gift for a friend or family member!

Supply List

- jar with a lid
- colored sand
- picture
- clear packing tape
- square piece of fabric
- rubber band
- scissors
- ribbon

1. Fill the jar with two or more colors of sand. Take turns adding a little bit of each color. Keep adding sand until the jar is completely full. Screw on the lid.

2. Choose a picture. Make sure it's small enough to fit on the side of the jar.

3. Cut a piece of tape a little longer than the picture is wide. Lay the tape down with the sticky side up. Lay the picture face down on the tape. Make sure the tape shows around the top and sides of the picture. Press the picture onto the tape. It's okay if the bottom of the picture is not on the tape.

4. Set the jar on its side. Turn the picture face up and lay it on the jar. Carefully smooth the tape around the jar. Cut another piece of tape to cover the bottom of the picture.

19

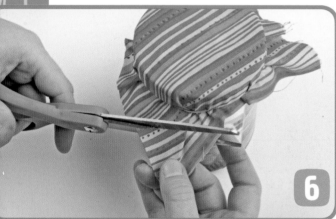

5 Put the **fabric** square over the top of the jar. Make sure it's big enough to completely cover the lid. Put a rubber band over the fabric to hold it on the jar.

6 Cut the fabric around the jar. Leave about ½ to 1 inch (1 to 3 cm) sticking out.

7 Cover the rubber band with a ribbon. Tie it in a bow!

More Super Ideas

Instead of colored sand, try these things.

shells

pasta

beans

Magic Mosaic Jar

A colorful jar for keeping little treasures!

Supply List

- jar with or without a lid
- 3 colors of polymer clay
- wax paper
- cookie sheet
- aluminum foil

1. If the lid needs to be painted, follow the steps on page 7.

2. Put the clay on a piece of wax paper. **Squeeze** the clay over and over until it is soft and stretchy.

3. Roll the clay into balls the size of peas. Make some balls out of each color of clay.

4. Press a ball of clay onto the jar. Push it flat so that it sticks and spreads out.

5. Add more balls of clay. The balls should touch each other. Keep adding balls of clay until the jar is covered. If the jar has a lid, don't cover the jar's **thread** with clay. If it doesn't have a lid, put clay all the way to the rim.

6. Put aluminum foil on a cookie sheet. Set the jar on the aluminum foil. Ask an adult to bake the jar according to the directions on the clay package. Do not bake the lid! Let the jar cool.

Nature Light

See how pretty this candleholder looks when it glows!

Supply List

- jar without a lid
- glue
- spoon
- small bowl
- tissue paper
- foam paintbrush
- pressed flowers and leaves (follow the steps on page 27)
- candle

1. Put 2 spoonfuls of glue into a small bowl. Add 2 spoonfuls of water. Mix the glue and water together.

2. Tear different colors of tissue paper into small pieces.

3. Use the foam paintbrush to cover part of the jar with the glue **mixture**.

4. Stick the tissue paper onto the glue. Repeat step 3 until the entire jar is covered with tissue paper. The pieces of tissue paper should overlap.

5 Brush on more glue. Add a second layer of tissue paper.

6 Glue on decorations such as leaves and flowers. Make it look pretty!

7 Cover the whole jar with the glue **mixture**. You might need to make more.

8 Wait for the glue to dry completely. Then ask an adult to put a candle inside the jar and light it. See how it glows!

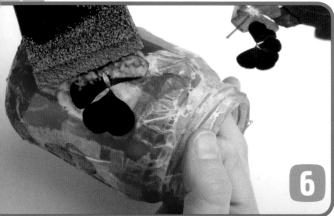

Press your own flowers and leaves!

1. Collect different leaves and flowers. Ask an adult before cutting a flower or leaf off of a plant.

2. Find a table or area of floor that is out of the way. Cover the surface with a sheet of newspaper. Lay the flowers and leaves on the newspaper. Make sure they don't touch each other.

3. Cover them with another sheet of newspaper.

4. Lay a heavy book on top of the newspaper.

5. Leave the flowers and leaves under the book for a week. Then remove the book and newspaper. The flowers and leaves will be pressed flat!

Super Snow Globe

This globe sparkles with falling snow!

1. Check your jar to make sure it doesn't **leak**. Follow the instructions on page 6.

2. If the lid needs to be painted, follow the steps on page 7.

3. Choose an object to go inside your snow globe. Try a plastic toy or figure. Make sure it fits inside the jar with the lid closed.

4. Press some florist's clay onto the middle of the lid. Make sure the center of the mound of clay is at least as tall as the lid. Spread the clay up to the edges of the lid.

5. Press the object firmly into the clay. Check to make sure the object is in the right spot. Set the jar on the lid to see how it looks. This is your last chance to move things around!

6 Set the jar in the kitchen sink. Pour mineral oil into the jar. Do not fill it all the way to the top. Lower the lid onto the jar, but don't screw it on yet. The object will make the level of the oil rise. Add or remove oil until it comes up to the bottom of the **thread**. You might want to ask an adult to help you. When the oil level is right, set the lid aside.

7 Now add the snow! Put glitter and confetti into the jar. Add a little bit at a time. Stir it to see how it looks. Be careful not to put in too much glitter. That could make it hard to see the figure.

8 Screw the lid onto the jar. Ask an adult to make sure that it's on **really** tight. Shake the jar and watch the snow **sparkle** and **whirl**!

More Super Ideas

Try using different toys or making a holiday theme.

Fourth of July

pirate

fairy

Glossary

design – a decorative pattern or arrangement.

fabric – woven material or cloth.

leak – to have a crack or hole that lets something in or out.

marshmallow – a soft, spongy kind of white candy.

mixture – a combination of two or more different things.

project – a task or activity.

really – very or very much.

slot – a narrow opening.

sparkle – to shine with flashes of light.

squeeze – to press the sides of something together.

thread – the ridge that winds around a screw or the top of a jar.

whirl – to move quickly in circles.

About SUPER SANDCASTLE™

**Bigger Books for Emerging Readers
Grades K–4**

Created for library, classroom, and at-home use, Super SandCastle™ books support and engage young readers as they develop and build literacy skills and will increase their general knowledge about the world around them. Super SandCastle™ books are an extension of SandCastle™, the leading preK–3 imprint for emerging and beginning readers. Super SandCastle™ features a larger trim size for more reading fun.

Let Us Know

Super SandCastle™ would like to hear your stories about reading this book. What was your favorite page? Was there something hard that you needed help with? Share the ups and downs of learning to read. We want to hear from you! Send us an e-mail.

sandcastle@abdopublishing.com

Contact us for a complete list of SandCastle™, Super SandCastle™, and other nonfiction and fiction titles from ABDO Publishing Company.

www.abdopublishing.com • 8000 West 78th Street
Edina, MN 55439 • 800-800-1312 • 952-831-1632 fax